Improving Design in the High Street

Colin J Davis

An RFAC guide
sponsored by
Department of the Environment
Land Securities
Marks & Spencer

published by
Architectural Press

Architectural Press

An imprint of Butterworth-Heinemann
Linacre House, Jordan Hill, Oxford OX2 8DP
A division of the Reed Educational and
Professional Publishing Ltd

℞ A member of the Reed Elsevier plc group

OXFORD BOSTON JOHANNESBURG
MELBOURNE NEW DELHI SINGAPORE

First published 1997
© Royal Fine Art Commission 1997

British Library Cataloguing in Publication Data
A catalogue record for this book is available from
the British Library

ISBN 0 7506 3453 7

Library of Congress Cataloguing in Publication Data
A catalogue record for this book is available from
the Library of Congress

Printed and bound in Great Britain

Improving Design in the High Street

Landmarks, part of high street character,

*are accentuated by a good foreground
(see page 72)*

Contents

Foreword by
Rt Hon.
John Gummer MP,
Secretary of State
for the
Environment

For centuries our town and city centres have provided the focus for so much of urban life - for living, shopping, leisure, civic activities or simply for meeting and mixing. Yet we cannot take their well being for granted. Today they face real challenges. They must respond to the changing needs and demands of modern-day living if they are to survive. They must provide places which are attractive and welcoming. They must compete effectively with out-of-town and edge-of-town developments.

At their best, traditional high streets offer both convenience and a real sense of place and character. Yet too often - and too easily - their defining identity has been spoilt through insensitive or careless action. We all appreciate fine buildings, quality public spaces or an intricate street pattern, yet will we readily return to a place where the streets are dirty, the car parks dingy and the pavements cluttered and ill-kempt?

We need a way to understand, and to act on, a high street's strengths and weaknesses - to accentuate the positive and deal effectively with the negative. This book explains in straightforward language how to identify the defining visual characteristics of a high street. It shows that it is often the small things that, cumulatively, can have such a marked impact on the quality of urban environment. Most importantly, it shows how, through a programme of action, qualities of convenience and character can be improved. That is not only good in itself but improves competitiveness and attracts further business and investment.

The Royal Fine Art Commission recognise the importance of our high streets. This book is but one example of their continuing work to promote quality in our built environment, a theme central to my own Department's Quality in Town and Country Initiative. It should stimulate and encourage others to consider how their own high street can be enhanced, adapting ideas to reflect its particular character and needs. Imposing a universal blueprint only leads to dull uniformity, unfortunately so often a hallmark of purpose-built centres.

There is a tremendous desire and enthusiasm in towns and cities up and down the country to see that our high streets are places of quality - and that they remain at the very heart of urban life. We all share a responsibility for their well being - as Government, central and local; as retailers, developers, investors and business generally; and as citizens of the local community. What is needed, therefore, is a practical programme of action, reflecting co-ordination and partnership between all involved. I, therefore, hope this book will be widely read and commend it as a valuable contribution to helping to show what can be done to improve our high streets.

Secretary of State for the Environment

Introduction

Design in the High Street, published by the Commission in 1986, sent out a clear message about better design and advocated its realisation through improved town centre management.

Ten years later, the wisdom of this message has been acknowledged. Yet many town centres and their high streets are still struggling. Further action is needed.

This book describes a straightforward method of analysing the design qualities of a town centre: what is good and what needs improving. It explains how a programme of co-ordinated action, based on this analysis, can benefit any town centre.

It is not intended to provide an explanation of comprehensive urban design analysis, although many of the techniques and issues highlighted are relevant to such analysis. Nor is it about the part that major redevelopment can play in achieving quality in town centres. Instead, the main focus is on the contribution that more modest and practical action can make to the improvement of the quality of the existing streetscape.

Practical examples of successful action, from towns and cities throughout the country, are seen from the viewpoint of elected members of local authorities. It is their enthusiasm and determination, and that of the local community more generally, which can be decisive in making the very best of their own town centre.

The High Street today and how it can be improved

It is by their centres that most towns are remembered. These centres of commerce in village, town or city tell the story of urban development and indicate the varying prosperity of the place through the ages.

Towns were seldom designed and built at one time: they have grown, been extended, altered or torn down according to the needs, the fashion and the prosperity of the day.

A total lack of uniformity is almost always the rule; the resultant mixture of the styles and materials contributes to the richness of our town centres... The town centre is the treasury of its current prosperity and also of its heritage.

Design in the High Street, Gordon Michell, Architectural Press/RFAC, 1986.

Town centres in competition

The words opposite, written ten years ago by Gordon Michell, introduced the Royal Fine Art Commission's previous publication on this subject. The comment is just as useful today, as town centres come to terms with changing circumstances at the end of the twentieth century.

Town centres need to prosper to survive. They have always faced a degree of competition from their neighbours but in the last ten or twenty years competition has increased markedly.

First, the growth in the number of out of town shopping centres and retail parks presents even greater choice for people with the ability to reach them. Secondly, potential customers, through greater personal mobility, are now able to choose between several centres.

Regardless of local intentions, our traditional town centres and their high streets are in a state of constant competition. Yet they often have distinct advantages over their out of town competitors. While purpose built centres can compete in terms of convenience they can seldom, if ever, match the best town centres in terms of distinctiveness, identity, quality of townscape: in short, their sense of place.

Traditional high streets can succeed if they play to these strengths. By providing an attractive environment and excellent design quality, as well as outstanding facilities, they can do a great deal to meet the ever increasing expectations of their customers and visitors.

PPG 6

The Government is understandably concerned to sustain and enhance the vitality and viability of town centres. Its Planning Policy Guidance Note *Town Centres and Retail Development* (PPG6, 1996) emphasises the need to regenerate our city, town and district centres.

PPG6 recommends focussing new development, especially retailing, in town centres, and encourages mixed-use development and coherent parking strategies as part of a programme to revitalise town centres. It also promotes the concept of town centre management and encourages good urban design as a way to improve the town centre environment and make it more attractive to visitors.

PPG6 suggests that local planning authorities should undertake an urban design analysis in order to provide a framework for policies in their development plan, and to help inform preparation of an action plan for improvements.

Underlying this advice is the notion that quality of environment and quality of service are essential for economic viability.

A process for improvement: analysis, programme, action

The Commission endorses the approach outlined in PPG6. Furthermore, it believes that every town centre can benefit from a process in which systematic analysis leads to a programme of co-ordinated action, as outlined on the following pages. This straightforward process, which is less than (but complementary to) a comprehensive urban design analysis, can be undertaken with benefit at any stage in the development plan cycle. The aim is to achieve practical improvements to the character and convenience of a town centre.

The aim of an initial **analysis** of a town centre should be to identify its qualities, of character as well as convenience, as described on pages 10-19. It should highlight what is good and what needs to be improved.

The sample analyses on pages 20-27 show how this approach can be applied to any town centre. Out of this analysis comes a **programme** of co-ordinated action.

Twenty five examples of successful **action** are given on pages 28-79.

These examples are included to provide some ideas about the sort of practical, and often modest, action which can make a real contribution to improving the quality of the existing townscape. In developing a programme of action, care needs to be taken to ensure that it is tailored to meet the specific needs of the local area.

Part I
Analysis of town centre quality and what to look for

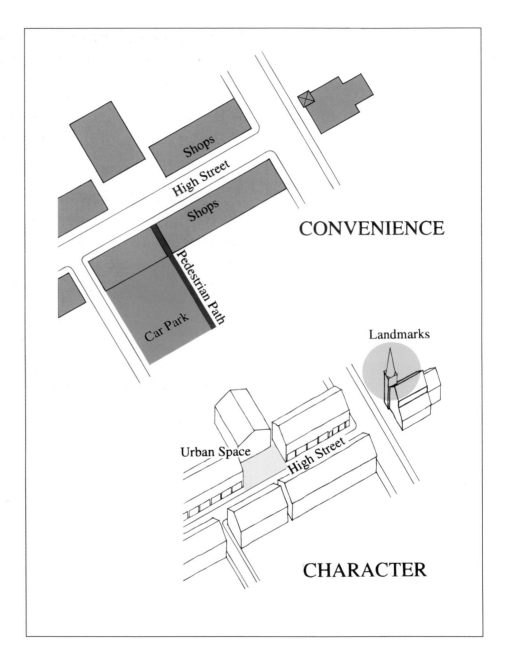

CONVENIENCE

CHARACTER

The process of improving a high street starts with an analysis of town centre quality, covering both its convenience and character.

Qualities of convenience include aspects such as car parking, directions, paths to the high street and the upkeep of the local environment.

Aspects of character include paving and street furniture, shop designs, the spatial proportions of streets and urban spaces, street life and local landmarks which help define the individual identity of a town centre. And, of course, they also include the character of the buildings themselves.

Each of these aspects is important in determining whether a town centre is an attractive, convenient place. Systematic analysis using a checklist can identify the places where improvements can be made.

Analysing the convenience of a town centre

CHECKLIST

Qualities of convenience	Action to improve convenience

WELCOME
Are car and bus passengers looked after?
Are drivers made welcome?
Do they feel safe as they leave the car?
Do people have to pass ugly back yards?
Is it easy to find your way?

1. Tidy up car park entrances
2. Make car park interiors welcoming
3. Integrate paths to the high street
4. Clarify pedestrian direction signs

A CARED FOR PLACE
Is the general impression good?
Are there torn flyposters?
Is there too much litter?
Are recycling waste bins unsightly?

5. Eliminate flyposters and graffiti
6. Clear litter & rubbish
7. Position waste recycling bins

COMFORT AND SAFETY
Are there pedestrian and traffic conflicts?
Is it difficult to cross the roads?

8. Calm traffic

Numbers refer to examples in Part III

The convenience of a town centre is relatively straightforward to measure. The checklist opposite lists some useful questions which can help in judging whether a town centre is safe, welcoming and attractive to visitors.

Very often, a car park, bus stop or bus station is where a visitor will concentrate on his surroundings for the first time or be able to take a longer critical look. These first impressions should be positive.

For example, traffic direction signs should be clear to first time visitors. The inside of multi-storey car parks should be light and airy, to encourage a feeling of security. Exits should be inviting and reachable via clean, safe and clearly marked routes.

The state of the path from the car park or bus station into the town centre is also important. Clear direction signs and pleasant paths reduce the apparent distance between car park and the high street. The way in which graffiti, litter and even recycled waste are dealt with helps create the impression that a town centre is cared for.

Convenience

Qualities of convenience

Are drivers made welcome?	(1)
Do they feel safe as they leave the car?	(2)
Do people have to pass ugly back yards?	(3)
Is it easy to find your way?	(4)
Are there torn flyposters?	(5)
Is there too much litter?	(6)
Are recycling waste bins unsightly?	(7)
Is it difficult to cross the roads?	(8)

Numbers refer to examples in Part III

At the high street, pedestrians may find traffic a nuisance, especially if it gets in the way of their logical direct path.

A scale plan, opposite, can be used as part of the analysis to help clarify the distances people need to walk to reach the high street and the detours they might have to take to find a safe route.

The plan would also show where the shops are, the busy traffic routes and the location of public spaces such as squares and parks.

Analysing character in town centres

CHECKLIST

Qualities of character	**Action to enhance character**
PAVEMENTS	
Are there local building materials?	
Do pavements match building quality?	9. Specify quality pavements
Are pavements cluttered?	10. Reduce street furniture clutter
Is street furniture well designed?	11. Rationalise traffic street furniture
SHOPS	
Do shopfronts relate to whole buildings?	
Is there a local design tradition or style?	12. Improve shopfronts
Do vacant shops deaden shopping parades?	13. Reduce impact of vacant shopfronts
Do shopsigns contribute to the street?	14. Relate shopsigns
URBAN SPACE	
What is street frontage height to width?	
Are there any gaps in the street frontage?	15. Design infill development
Is there potential for new urban space?	16. Create incidental urban space
Would trees be an asset?	17. Plant street trees
Will a splash of colour enhance the street?	18. Introduce seasonal colour
STREET LIFE	
Is there more to do than just shop?	
Is there a lively street market?	19. Encourage market stalls
Are the urban spaces used fully?	20. Vary activities in urban spaces
Is there a community or cultural tradition?	21. Establish special events
LOCAL LANDMARKS	
What are the true local landmarks?	
What are the short and long views to/from?	22. Accentuate landmarks
Do landmarks need to be emphasised?	23. Design paving for special places
Should landmarks be enhanced at night?	24. Install public lighting
Should local interests be celebrated?	25. Place art in public places

Numbers refer to examples in Part III

Character can often be difficult to describe and analyse. In undertaking this part of the analysis, it might help to consult people who have a special understanding of the architecture and history of a place.

Although the checklist opposite does not specifically consider the character and quality of the buildings themselves, even the simplest analysis should highlight prominent or recurring architectural features or building forms. A distinct architectural style might have resulted from the town's history.

The checklist draws attention to various aspects of character, such as pavements and street furniture. Local traditional paving, used because of its availability and durability, can often be seen in private courts near a high street, even if it has disappeared from the high street itself.

Apart from fulfilling practical purposes, street furniture can enhance a high street. At the very least it should not add to unsightly clutter, which often hides the individuality of a town's character. Traffic signs and structures, including yellow lines, must conform to national standards but need not be too intrusive.

The design of shopfronts and shopsigns can enhance the character of a town by using local styles and craftsmanship and by relating visually to the whole building. And the management of empty shopfronts can reduce their impact on the attractiveness of a high street.

Character

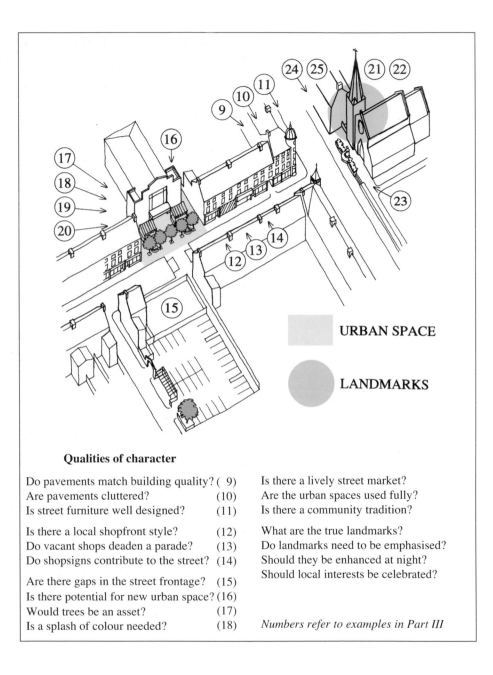

URBAN SPACE

LANDMARKS

Qualities of character

Do pavements match building quality? (9)
Are pavements cluttered? (10)
Is street furniture well designed? (11)

Is there a local shopfront style? (12)
Do vacant shops deaden a parade? (13)
Do shopsigns contribute to the street? (14)

Are there gaps in the street frontage? (15)
Is there potential for new urban space? (16)
Would trees be an asset? (17)
Is a splash of colour needed? (18)

Is there a lively street market?
Are the urban spaces used fully?
Is there a community tradition?

What are the true landmarks?
Do landmarks need to be emphasised?
Should they be enhanced at night?
Should local interests be celebrated?

Numbers refer to examples in Part III

Character is also influenced by the scale of a street, that is its total width compared with the height of the buildings which line it. Changes in these proportions along a street, between a main street and minor streets and at an urban space such as a town square help us to recognise a place. These qualities may be understood more clearly through a perspective sketch, opposite.

Distant views across to a town centre, views from a street into an urban space or just straight at a monument or landmark are remembered and appreciated as features which help to give a place its identity.

Street life in the form of community activities, special events or simply a street market add to the local flavour of a town centre, providing interest and incidental free entertainment for the visitor.

If we are to make the most of our high streets, we must understand what gives them their character. Asking the questions in the checklist can help to pinpoint each high street's individual qualities, as well as identifying its needs and revealing opportunities for improvement. Better open spaces, seasonal colour, an improved setting for local life and activities, better lighting and art in public places might all be used to enhance character.

Part II
Sample analyses leading to programmes of co-ordinated action

Examples which could form part of a programme of co-ordinated action

Qualities of convenience	Action to improve convenience
WELCOME	1. Tidy up car park entrances
	2. Make car park interiors welcoming
	3. Integrate paths to the high street
	4. Clarify pedestrian direction signs
A CARED FOR PLACE	5. Eliminate flyposters and graffiti
	6. Clear litter and rubbish
	7. Position waste recycling bins
COMFORT AND SAFETY	8. Calm traffic

Qualities of character	Action to enhance character
PAVEMENTS	9. Specify quality pavements
	10. Reduce street furniture clutter
	11. Rationalise traffic street furniture
SHOPS	12. Improve shopfronts
	13. Reduce impact of vacant shopfronts
	14. Relate shopsigns
URBAN SPACE	15. Design infill development
	16. Create incidental urban space
	17. Plant street trees
	18. Introduce seasonal colour
STREET LIFE	19. Encourage market stalls and kiosks
	20. Vary activities in urban spaces
	21. Establish special events
LOCAL LANDMARKS	22. Accentuate landmarks
	23. Design paving for special places
	24. Install public lighting
	25. Place art in public places

Numbers refer to examples in Part III

Once the high street has been analysed to decide what is good and what needs improving, the next step is to put together a programme of co-ordinated action. To be effective, this is likely to require co-operation and input from a number of agencies and funding programmes. Specific examples of co-operation and funding methods are given in Part III.

The process of analysis leading to the preparation of programmes of co-ordinated action would benefit any town centre, making it more convenient for visitors and enhancing its character.

In the following pages of sample analyses, we take three typical high streets - in a market town, an inner city centre and a sub-regional centre - and show how a programme of co-ordinated action would be tailored to fit each of them.

The samples are only intended to illustrate how the process would apply to different high streets. They do not presume to have taken into account all the priorities for the particular town centres.

Bridgnorth

The small market town of Bridgnorth, Shropshire, is in competition with larger shopping centres and out of town retail parks. Because it is not large enough to attract many national high street names, goods are provided in the main through local retailers. Most shoppers arrive by car, so parking facilities are essential. In these respects Bridgnorth's problems are similar to those of hundreds of small town and suburban centres.

The town is only twenty minutes' driving time from the large centres of Shrewsbury and Wolverhampton. Its main purpose is to serve the local community.

Convenience
In the high street there are bus stops and some short term free parking. The main car parks, which are surface level, are some distance from the shops and this is perhaps the greatest difficulty and inconvenience for shoppers.

Some of the approaches to the car parks and the walks to the shop could usefully be improved but graffiti and rubbish are not a problem.

Traffic is light in the high street but fast enough to cause difficulties for the elderly or people with disabilities.

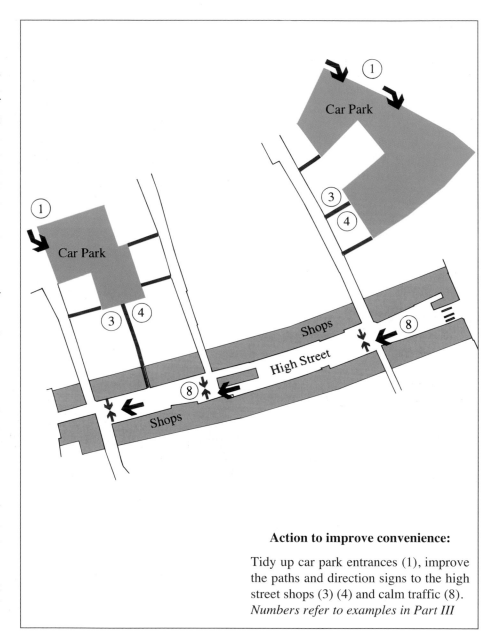

Action to improve convenience:

Tidy up car park entrances (1), improve the paths and direction signs to the high street shops (3) (4) and calm traffic (8). *Numbers refer to examples in Part III*

Character

From the eastern approach to the town there are spectacular views across the river to the hilltop town.

The wide high street, an urban space, is visually enclosed at both ends by the medieval town gates. It is a powerful visual asset. Narrow streets lead off to other urban spaces and landmarks such as churches, steep hills and long runs of steps.

There is already a busy street life and special events enrich the town and attract new visitors.

Action to enhance character would emphasise the feel of an historic town not only in the high street but back to the car parks. The design of infill development should respect and enhance the subtle variations in urban spaces.

The clarity of the high street shape should not be compromised by street furniture clutter.

Local traditional clay paviors should be used for pavements, access drives, gutters and the long runs of steps.

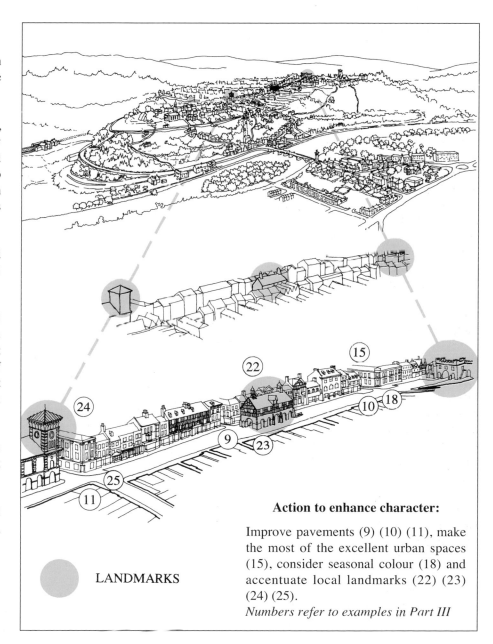

LANDMARKS

Action to enhance character:

Improve pavements (9) (10) (11), make the most of the excellent urban spaces (15), consider seasonal colour (18) and accentuate local landmarks (22) (23) (24) (25).
Numbers refer to examples in Part III

Brixton

Brixton, about three miles from the centre of London, is a town centre in its own right. Like many English city neighbourhoods, it has evolved from rural hamlet to smart Victorian suburb and is now a multicultural place with a twenty four hour life.

Its high street has to cope with heavy traffic. And although there is a thriving street market, it is the sort of place where much effort is needed to avoid inner city decay. As such, it is reasonably typical of many secondary centres in the large conurbations.

Convenience

Most people arrive by bus or tube right in the middle of the high street.

Local people walk in from all directions, past the car parks and commercial back yards. As in many inner city areas, there are considerable problems in maintaining a cared for appearance.

The high street carries heavy through traffic, causing great difficulties for pedestrians.

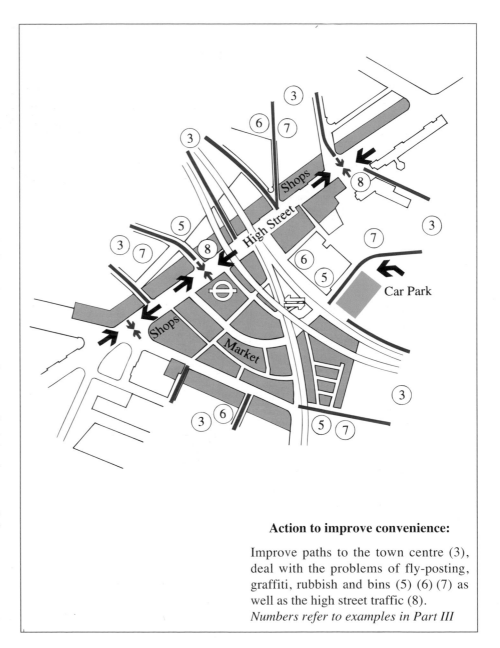

Action to improve convenience:

Improve paths to the town centre (3), deal with the problems of fly-posting, graffiti, rubbish and bins (5) (6) (7) as well as the high street traffic (8).
Numbers refer to examples in Part III

Character

This is possibly the most difficult type of centre to analyse. Even the traffic, though it causes problems, adds to the bustle and sense of vitality. Street life is vibrant and varied.

The landmarks are a surprising asset: the double railway bridges and a few excellent Victorian buildings help to provide an identity. The high street has small public gardens and contrasting areas of wide pavement, both of which are important to street life.

There is a marked difference in scale between the wide high street and the narrow side streets, with their small shops and market stalls.

Action to enhance character would accentuate the landmarks by improving their foreground setting through good quality pavements and the reduction of street clutter.

The contrast between areas of different character and scale can be emphasised through shopfront and shopsign design.

There may be opportunities to create new incidental urban spaces and to consider appropriate places to plant street trees.

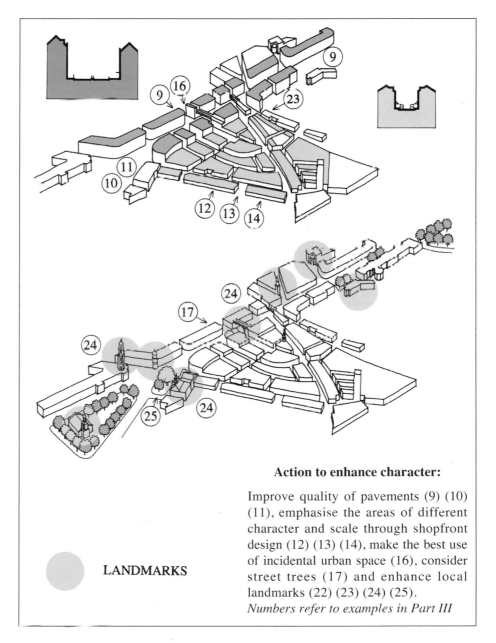

LANDMARKS

Action to enhance character:

Improve quality of pavements (9) (10) (11), emphasise the areas of different character and scale through shopfront design (12) (13) (14), make the best use of incidental urban space (16), consider street trees (17) and enhance local landmarks (22) (23) (24) (25).
Numbers refer to examples in Part III

Leicester

Leicester has successfully adapted to changing circumstances ever since it was laid out by the Romans. It is now a major sub-regional shopping centre combining all the functions of a city and county town; to remain so, it must provide the very best modern facilities.

As the city centre has been adapted to modern standards, many streets in the core shopping area have been pedestrianised and now link into historic and modern shopping malls. There is a large area of covered and open interconnecting spaces where people can walk safely.

Convenience

As one would expect in a thriving centre, customer convenience is being continually reviewed. City buses stop outside the shops. Car parks are so located that people can walk directly from them into the shopping malls and pedestrianised streets.

Action to improve convenience would concentrate on standards of comfort and safety in and around the multi-storey car parks.

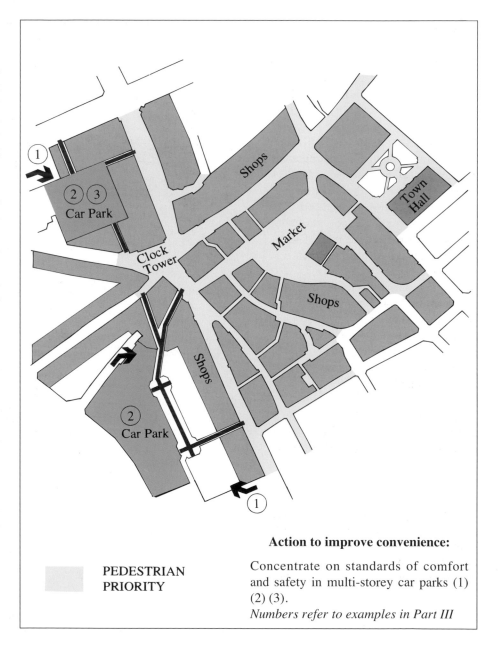

PEDESTRIAN PRIORITY

Action to improve convenience:

Concentrate on standards of comfort and safety in multi-storey car parks (1) (2) (3).
Numbers refer to examples in Part III

Character

Important landmarks such as the town hall, a Victorian clock tower and a large thriving covered market help provide identity.

Road closures and pedestrianisation schemes in the city centre have created a pattern of urban spaces and narrow passages, open or covered but each with an individual size or shape.

Redevelopment has tended to respect this pattern, so that the distinction between spaces is retained.

Action to enhance character would continue to emphasise the interesting differences between each urban space, through infill development, details of paving and street furniture as well as a variety of activities.

Programmes of activities, community events or commercial promotions could be organised to suit different spaces.

The design and maintenance of paving for special public places and even small kiosks is important. These details are noticed by visitors entering the public spaces from the privately managed shopping arcades.

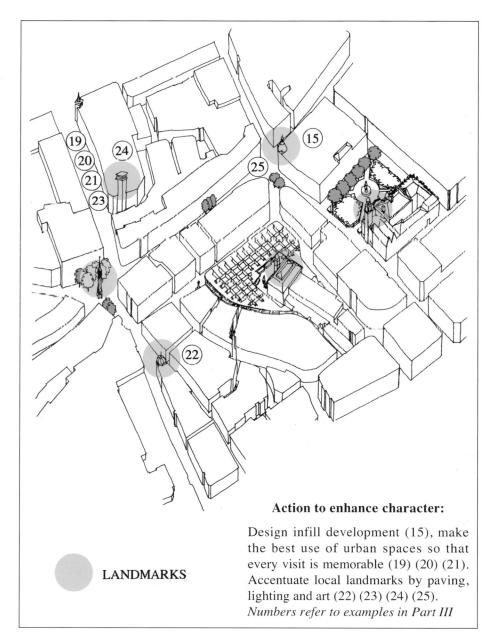

LANDMARKS

Action to enhance character:

Design infill development (15), make the best use of urban spaces so that every visit is memorable (19) (20) (21). Accentuate local landmarks by paving, lighting and art (22) (23) (24) (25).
Numbers refer to examples in Part III

Part III
Action:
How town centres
have been improved

On the following pages, we list twenty five ways in which a high street can be improved and give examples of how each of our suggestions can be made to work in practice. Once the needs of a town centre have been identified by means of an analysis, this list can be used to construct a tailored programme of co-ordinated action.

ACTION	LOCATION
WELCOME	
1. Tidy up car park entrances	Canterbury
2. Make car park interiors welcoming	Lincoln
3. Integrate paths to the high street	Altrincham
4. Clarify pedestrian direction signs	Edinburgh
A CARED FOR PLACE	
5. Eliminate flyposters and graffiti	Wolverhampton
6. Clear litter and rubbish	Coventry
7. Position waste recycling bins	Kensington & Chelsea
COMFORT AND SAFETY	
8. Calm traffic	Borehamwood
PAVEMENTS	
9. Specify quality pavements	Halifax
10. Reduce street furniture clutter	City of London
11. Rationalise traffic street furniture	Hartlepool
SHOPS	
12. Improve shopfronts	Bootle
13. Reduce impact of vacant shopfronts	Barnsley
14. Relate shopsigns	Godalming
URBAN SPACE	
15. Design infill development	Bromley
16. Create incidental urban space	Notting Hill Gate
17. Plant street trees	Cheltenham
STREET LIFE	
18. Introduce seasonal colour	Devizes etc
19. Encourage market stalls and kiosks	Wigan
20. Vary activities in urban spaces	Hereford
21. Establish special events	Bridgnorth
LOCAL LANDMARKS	
22. Accentuate landmarks	Brixton
23. Design paving for special places	Westminster
24. Install public lighting	Leeds
25. Place art in public places	Sunderland

The list is certainly not intended to be comprehensive: there are many other ways in which town centres can be improved. Our purpose is to provide practical ideas for others to consider in their own area with suitable modifications to reflect local conditions.

The examples highlight some useful lessons from general experience.

First, co-operation and a co-ordinated approach are essential. A successful programme of action depends on different agencies and organisations agreeing a set of shared objectives and working together to achieve them.

These objectives are best identified through a formal process of analysis. This is essential in a small town like Bridgnorth, which is managed by three tiers of local government - county, district and town council.

Secondly, many of the problems facing the high street require long term action and a commitment to carry out change over time. That is not to imply, of course, that little can be done to improve a town centre in the short term.

Many examples cited in this book can, with effective partnership, be carried out relatively quickly and often within modest budgets.

A strategy for action is required, covering both short and long term, which is achievable and has the support and commitment of those involved.

A third underlying message is that although local authority funds are usually targeted at specific services, rather than at a town centre as a whole, it is often possible to link funds. Several of our examples show how this can be done.

At Borehamwood, for example, traffic calming was funded by both county and district councils, while at Coventry a new city centre company has been established, funded by a mix of public and private finance.

In our examples we give an outline of the context, notes on implementation and funding and a personal message from a representative of the authority or organisation primarily involved. In each case a contact name is provided for further advice and information.

CONTEXT

The first example is a simple sign and entrance to a car park. These signs need to be seen clearly by drivers without appearing over fussy or cluttered in the street scene. At Castle Street, Canterbury, the signs only face the direction of traffic.

The car park entrance is fitted into the design of the houses and respects the scale and architectural rhythm of the street. It is similar in design to a traditional domestic vehicle entrance.

The upper sketch, as a comparison, gives an idea of how large bulky car parks can overpower and dominate the scale of a street. The lower sketch is a reminder of the unattractive entrances to some town centre car parks.

Car park entrances and their signs can be sensitively fitted into a street scene

IMPLEMENTATION AND FUNDING

The car park signs and car park entrance were designed to fit the street scene. It was possible to integrate them with the buildings along the street because the local authority is responsible for both off street car parks and public housing.

People arriving at a town centre by car need to have clear directions to guide them safely to a convenient car park.
These signs should be fitted neatly into the setting of the town so that they do not appear cluttered or shabby.
Our policy is to foster economic well being by taking as much care with small details in our city centre, such as car park signs, shopfronts and shopsigns, as we do with large developments.

Councillor Professor Clive Wake
Lord Mayor
Canterbury City Council

Contact: John Chater
Assistant Director, Planning
Tel. 01227 763763

Tidy up car park entrances

1

Signs for drivers and the entrance to a car park behind a row of houses in Castle Street, Canterbury, have been designed to respect the scale and materials of the historic street.

CONTEXT

The quality of the whole town centre might be judged by the standards of its car parks. Many older multi-storey car parks were built when people were prepared to accept lower space and comfort standards. Now, efficiency and convenience are expected. Equally important are cleanliness and lightness.

The inside of a car park, in particular, needs to be clean, light and safe. It is here that a driver becomes a pedestrian and begins to see his surroundings through different eyes.

It helps if drivers can see a safe place to walk towards before they leave their cars.

The inside of a car park, in particular, needs to be clean, light and safe

IMPLEMENTATION AND FUNDING
The car park was funded as part of a mixed use shopping development.

Ceiling heights are eleven feet instead of six or seven and the lighting almost equals that of an office. The colour scheme, spacing of columns and CCTV increase the sense of space, light and safety.

We were keen to have a most safe and convenient car park that would serve to revive the whole area.
Given the historic location, design was crucial. Not only did the car park have to form part of the urban fabric, it had to project an image of safety.
In this car park you can see clearly to the shops and streets, on-site management is available and cameras are installed.
The past image of decked car parks is poor. Lincoln shows by example that it does not need to be.

Councillor Laurie Vaisey
Chairman of the Planning Committee
Lincoln City Council

Contact: Peter Harness
Senior Planning Officer
Tel. 01522 564475

Make interiors of car parks welcoming 2

A multi-storey car park at St. Mark's, in Lincoln city centre is designed to make users feel safe. It is very light, and has high ceilings and clear views. It has received a national Police Gold Award for secure car parks.

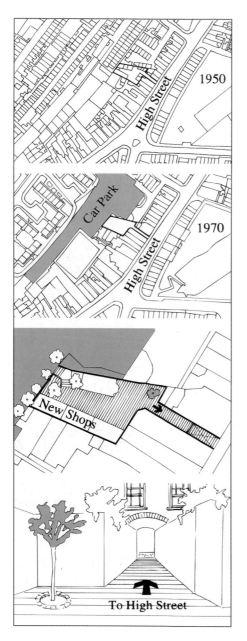

CONTEXT

Towns have to adapt to changing circumstances. Backland sites are often used for car parks and as a result are often cut off from the high street they serve. In many towns people have to pass dismal commercial back yards and narrow dark alleys on their way from the car park to the high street.

In Altrincham, where many of the high street shops had their own back yards and outbuildings with access from the high street, an improvement programme has been carried out over a period of twenty years.

First a car park was built on a back land site behind the high street shops. Then, when a yard was redeveloped, the opportunity was taken to provide a pedestrian route from the car park through the development to the high street.

People can now park in a surface car park, walk towards the welcoming entrance of a group of small shops in Kings Court and go through a pleasant courtyard on their way to the high street.

The car park and the path to the high street have been improved over twenty years

Integrate paths to the high street 3

IMPLEMENTATION AND FUNDING
The pedestrian link through to the high street and the initial landscaping in the car park were provided by the developer of Kings Court under a legal agreement.

Since then the introduction of car park attendants has provided a degree of official presence which reduces petty crime.

Ongoing maintenance of the car park surface and landscape is funded from pay and display charges.

When the site next to the car park was redeveloped in the 1980s we used planning powers to secure a new way through to Railway Street.
This, together with excellent car park maintenance, has helped to maintain the viability of the high street.

Councillor Beverley Hughes
Leader of the Council
Trafford Metropolitan Borough Council

Contact: Alan Hubbard
Principal Planner
Tel. 0161 912 4746

A development of small shops at Altrincham was specially designed as an interesting walk from a public car park to the high street shops at Railway Street. At Devizes, above, a similar path leads from the car park to the high street.

CONTEXT

Pedestrians have more time than drivers to find signs and read them. Unlike traffic signs, signs for pedestrians do not have to conform to national standards. There is therefore scope to make them more varied and interesting.

The sketches on the left show three arrangements of signs: fixed to a wall, formed out of tiles set into a brick wall, and carved into a stone pavement. Compared with the bottom sketch of a less considered free standing sign, they contribute to the quality of the street by providing information whilst not adding to the clutter of posts and structures.

The photograph opposite shows three signs on the same wall at a passage off a high street. They serve quite distinct groups of people with a subtlety that is impossible on a post mounted sign.

The topmost sign provides clear directions for tourists. The bottom sign assumes that the reader is a discerning visitor with time to spend. It gives a lengthy explanation of local history. And in the middle are the remains of an old commercial painted sign which, though of no practical use at present, is an essential part of the local character. It is a vivid reminder of the industry that once took place in the court.

A less thoughtful solution might have added to pavement clutter or obliterated the original commercial sign, thereby severing a real link with the past.

Signs for pedestrians can be interesting. Bottom left: what might have been

IMPLEMENTATION AND FUNDING
The direction signs were erected as part of a programme initiated by the Old Town Renewal Trust.

The old commercial signs were retained in the refurbishment of the adjacent court buildings.

Funding by the government-supported Renewal Trust on this and other related projects has brought to the Old Town new activities, expanding businesses and a steadily growing population.

Tourism makes a significant contribution to the prosperity of Edinburgh. Consequently, well designed direction signs are essential. As part of the Royal Mile Project, we put up signs which gave outline information about the area, as well as keeping old signs which offered some genuine reminders of the city's past.

Duncan Fraser
Central Area Manager
City of Edinburgh

Contact: Jon Mengham
Edinburgh Old Town Renewal Trust
Tel. 0131 225 8818

Clarify pedestrian direction signs

Direction signs for pedestrians need to be more subtle than those for drivers. These Edinburgh signs show a concern for the interests of first time tourists, discerning visitors and local people.

CONTEXT

Posters can provide useful information but their effectiveness is reduced when they are torn or randomly placed as flyposters.

The subliminal message of flyposters is dereliction. In some inner city high streets they can accumulate quickly to form a nucleus of decay around which other rubbish collects.

By contrast, most purpose built shopping centres are well managed, cleaned and regularly maintained. Flyposters and graffiti are not tolerated.

At Wolverhampton, flyposters and graffiti are generally steamed off and special varnishes are applied to vulnerable walls to make removal easier. Textured surfaces, whether applied as a paint, incorporated into the design of a structure or even provided by climbing plants, can also discourage flyposters.

The sketches on the left show how the removal of flyposters and graffiti combined with good structural maintenance (see page 58) can have a significant effect.

Removal of graffiti and flyposters combined with a simple robust boundary wall

Eliminate flyposters and graffiti

5

IMPLEMENTATION AND FUNDING
Flyposters and graffiti are regularly removed by a special task force which aims to remove them before they have been up for twenty four hours. This reduces their commercial value and discourages other people from fixing unlawful posters.

Funding is from the Highways and Transportation budget.

This work requires perseverance but the results are worthwhile. Visitors, including potential investors, notice the absence of flyposters and comment on the fact. It helps create a positive image for Wolverhampton and was one reason why we won the British Council of Shopping Centres Environmental Award in 1993.

Councillor Norman Davies OBE
Leader of the Council
Wolverhampton
Metropolitan Borough Council.

Contact: Ken Mackie
Town Centre Manager
Tel. 01902 315400

Flyposters and graffiti are removed quickly and effectively.

CONTEXT

The need to remove litter and rubbish is self evident.

Tolerance by the public of other people's rubbish has reduced in recent years as out of town and purpose built shopping arcades, where cleanliness is the norm, have become more common. High streets have to attain the same high standards and so clearing litter and rubbish has become a high priority.

The Environmental Protection Act 1990 allows local authorities to require certain businesses and landowners to clear litter from outside their premises. Use of these powers can help to create a cared for high street where individual characteristics can be appreciated.

The two sketches on the left show how smooth pavements (see page 46) and substantial boundary walls at the back of the pavement (see page 58) help to keep a town centre tidy.

Litter and rubbish are easier to clear from smooth and uncluttered pavements

Clear litter and rubbish

6

IMPLEMENTATION AND FUNDING
The Coventry City Centre Management Company, a joint venture with the private sector, is due to come into being in April 1997.

Funding is partly from the existing local authority city centre service budgets. Private sector contributions and E U Article 10 funding are also being sought.

We are convinced that the appearance of the city centre is an important factor for companies considering moving to Coventry.
People compare the city centre with purpose designed and well maintained shopping centres. They demand a cleaner, safer, more colourful, more lively and particularly a far better maintained city centre.
This has led the City Council to set up the new company, which is a considerable innovation in city centre management.

Liz Millett
Chief Executive
Coventry City Centre Management Co

Contact: Chris Beck, Asst. Director
City Development Directorate
Tel. 01203 833333

Litter and rubbish are cleared from Coventry city centre as part of a management programme funded through a new City Centre Company.

41

Waste recycling bins need to be well designed and sited, kept clean and maintained

CONTEXT

Unfortunately the sight of overflowing, damaged, dirty, poster strewn bins is common in many town centres. Often they are sited in car parks, at the place where people should be welcomed to a town centre. Unless very regularly emptied, they attract more rubbish which is piled up on the pavement next to them.

The current aims of recycling more waste, in pursuit of environmental goals, has led to a proliferation of large unsightly waste bins. Yet a cared for appearance is essential for the well being of a high street. This seeming conflict of objectives needs to be resolved.

Whatever the final destination of the contents, the receptacles are in reality large dustbins and as a consequence need to be well designed and sited, kept clean and maintained.

Some authorities collect certain categories of recyclable waste from houses and business premises. The example opposite shows this being done in Kensington & Chelsea using special lorries. The result is a reduction in the need for pavement bins.

IMPLEMENTATION AND FUNDING

As an alternative to bottle banks and large waste recycling bins, material is collected for recycling in special dual compartment vehicles.

Sorting is carried out by hand so that all the categories of recyclable waste are correctly identified. Funding is through normal refuse collection budgets.

This scheme was developed to reduce the necessity for so many street corner bottle banks. In a crowded part of London there are very few acceptable places to put recycling bins either in the high streets or residential areas.

Councillor Mrs Joan Hanham
Leader of the Council
Royal Borough of Kensington & Chelsea

Contact: Sharon Ross
Recycling Manager
Tel. 0171 341 5148

Position waste recycling bins

Waste for recycling is collected from each household and business premises in Kensington & Chelsea in special twin compartment vehicles. This reduces the need for so many pavement containers.

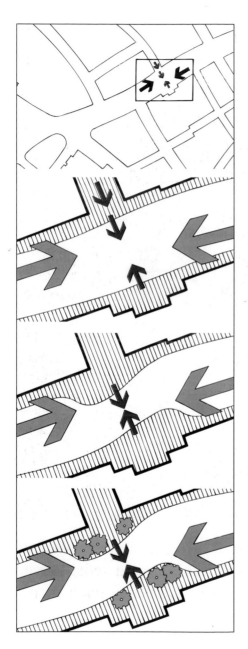

CONTEXT

Many high streets have to accept through traffic even though this leads to traffic / pedestrian conflicts. Sometimes pedestrianisation is not feasible, sometimes it is desirable to retain some traffic movement. The aim in urban design terms is to resolve these conflicts so that pedestrians can use the high street in safety and comfort.

Drivers are used to having priority over pedestrians, so calming traffic on main roads requires considerable changes to normal driver behaviour.

At the high street in Borehamwood, unofficial crossing places have been installed and are marked by raised surfaces across the carriageway. The frequency of these crossing places encourages careful driving and gives pedestrians sufficient safe places to cross. They are therefore unlikely to attempt to cross at other places. Barriers in the form of guard rails are unnecessary. Raised planters on the pavements help guide pedestrians to the crossing places.

In most similar high streets, official crossing places are reduced to a few designated locations. Pedestrians are then prevented (often by substantial steel barriers) from crossing at any other place. These barriers add considerably to the untidiness of many high streets.

Traffic calming measures can be fitted sensitively into the urban scene

IMPLEMENTATION AND FUNDING
The county highway authority worked closely with the district planning authority.

Finance was primarily from Sect. 106 planning gain funds, with some county highway funds and contributions from the district council.

Traffic is usually calmed in side streets. At Borehamwood we worked closely with Hertsmere Borough Council to calm the traffic in the main shopping street.
The unusual feature of this scheme is that drivers have been persuaded, without any special traffic regulations, to willingly give way to pedestrians, even at non-statutory crossing places and wave them across.
It was an experiment which has been more successful than we expected.

Brian York
Chairman of the Environment Cttee.
Hertfordshire County Council

Contact: Rob Smith
Head of Strategy & Implementation
Environment Dept.   Tel. 01992 556059

Calm traffic

Traffic is calmed in the high street at Borehamwood, reducing traffic speeds to a steady, calm and safe 20mph. Drivers willingly give way to pedestrians at each of the informal crossing places.

CONTEXT

Pavements form the foreground of virtually every urban scene. Their quality is therefore important.

Sometimes the potential for quality is lost because ordinary durable paving materials are not laid with sufficient care or are damaged by heavy vehicles. Alternatively, where additional funds are available, over-lavish paving schemes draw unnecessary attention to a pavement and thereby compete with rather than complement the view.

The most successful pavements are those which answer all the practical requirements of robustness but employ traditional materials to reflect a particular local character. For this it helps to research exactly what the traditional material is. In many towns, regularly used pavements will have been replaced several times since uniform standard concrete slabs became common. Traditional materials can probably still be seen in little-used streets and in private access drives, off the high street.

The two upper sketches on the left show a local engineering brick and pavior used for pavements, steps and even gutters at Bridgnorth, Shropshire. The third sketch shows a typical stone kerb and gutter as well as a stone sett carriageway, of the type used at Halifax (see facing page).

The picture of Halifax also shows experimental traffic signs, fitted with reflective faces instead of bulky lighting equipment. They were put up as part of a Department of Transport and English Historic Towns Forum initiative to reduce street clutter.

In some places, ordinary concrete slabs may be the most sensible paving surface. A similar scale and bond as York stone can be achieved relatively cheaply if large standard sized slabs are cut and laid with the same attention to detail that would be given to York stone (see bottom left).

Finally, a surface that is easy to keep clean obviously helps in clearing litter and rubbish (see page 40). If brick paviors or setts are used, joints should be be filled to avoid creating litter traps.

Local brick and stone. Concrete slabs are acceptable if well cut and laid

IMPLEMENTATION AND FUNDING

Funding was from highway maintenance and improvement budgets. As buses had been re-routed out of the street, maintenance was extended to include traffic calming and higher quality streets and pavements.

We took the opportunity to upgrade the highway and pavements in the Halifax Town Centre Conservation Area to complement the civic buildings, including the listed Town Hall.
Parking is controlled but by creating a Restricted Zone we have replaced the unsightly yellow lines with small signs, carefully placed on adjacent buildings.
In consultation with disability groups we have used special brass pavement studs which help blind people and are easy to lay and attractive, and flat topped speed tables which provide level crossing places.

Councillor Pam Warhurst
Leader of the Council
Calderdale Metropolitan Borough Council

Contact: Martin Brockie
Assistant Director, Technical Services
Tel. 01422 392168

Specify quality pavements

9

Traditional York stone paving slabs, recycled granite setts and new sawn sandstone setts have been used at Halifax to give durable and clean surfaces. Yellow lines have been replaced with carefully sited signs.

CONTEXT

Clutter on public pavements is an accumulation of seemingly essential structures. As high streets adapt to meet changing needs, pavements collect additional pieces of equipment and signs. Each no doubt has, or had, a purpose; but seen together, they merely form visual clutter which reduces the individuality of a town's character.

Signs, posts, brackets, barriers, bollards and coloured and textured paving often follow a standard national design and are placed with no regard to the surrounding buildings or to the visual composition of the street. Each category of street furniture in a street needs to be examined to see if there are other ways to carry out its purpose.

This example tackles just one category, lighting columns, and reduces clutter by fixing them to buildings. A special by-law for the Corporation of London (see note below) is one reason why it has been so successful. But with determination and a long term programme, other cities have achieved similar results in smaller areas.

The same care is needed in locating closed circuit television cameras, direction signs and supports for traffic signs.

Reducing clutter has a dramatic effect on the appearance of a high street. Landmark buildings can be appreciated more easily and the street appears to be more cared for.

The Corporation of London's 1900 by-law gives it power to "...affix to the external wall of any building fronting any street within the City any brackets wires pipes lamps and apparatus as may be necessary or convenient for the public lighting of the streets within the City."

One way to reduce street clutter is to fix street lights to buildings

Reduce street furniture clutter

10

IMPLEMENTATION AND FUNDING
In the City of London light fittings, equipment boxes and conduits are fixed neatly to or within buildings.

Normal street lighting budgets are used.

We take advantage of a by-law which allows us to insist on fixing public street lights to buildings.
This means that over the years we have been able to attain satisfactory street lighting while achieving very high standards of visual quality - essential to our status as the financial centre of Europe.
Pavement clutter is minimal.
The light fittings are fixed to historic and new buildings in relation to their various architectural features.
The advantages of obtaining a similar by-law could be considered by other authorities.

Mrs Barbara Newman, Chairman
Planning & Transportation Committee
Corporation of London

Contact: David Richards
Principal Engineer, Client Side
Tel. 0171 332 1894

In order to reduce street clutter, most of the street lights in the City of London are fixed neatly to buildings.

*To rationalise traffic street furniture,
each type is dealt with separately*

CONTEXT

The visual impact of street furniture should be reduced to the minimum compatible with fulfilling practical functions. Street furniture usually forms the foreground of a scene. Quality design and manufacture are essential.

Traffic related street furniture is probably the most difficult to deal with as each piece of equipment has a practical function, must conform to national standards and is often erected by different agencies at different times. For this reason it is very time consuming to achieve visual co-ordination.

In this example, a new traffic scheme requiring new traffic signals was co-ordinated with a landscape scheme for a public square in front of the Civic Centre. The opportunity was taken to reduce street furniture to a minimum and paint it all the same colour. Lamp columns, traffic signal posts and railings have all been painted black. The effect is tidy without appearing too fussy or twee.

The sketches on the left show how a similar street might look if there was not the same concern to rationalise traffic street furniture.

To achieve a similar effect elsewhere it would be necessary to adopt a straightforward policy to co-ordinate the colour of all street furniture, including traffic related equipment. Although there are limits to the range of acceptable alternative colours for traffic equipment, the procedure is worth following.

The visual clutter of painted signs and lines on roads can also be reduced. In certain circumstances the Department of Transport will give permission for waiting restriction yellow lines to be removed and replaced by signs. The example at Halifax, page 46, also shows some less obtrusive traffic signs being tested.

IMPLEMENTATION AND FUNDING
The work is being carried out as part of a programme to regenerate the centre of Hartlepool.

Funding is from a combination of Urban Programme, EU and City Challenge budgets. The success of the work has encouraged some local businesses to carry out their own redevelopments.

The quality of the street scene at the entrance to the Civic Centre sets the tone for the rest of the town centre.
We have used several budgets but made sure that the projects are dovetailed together to produce a total effect.
We are convinced that a co-ordinated approach is right. Co-ordination is essential if we are going to up-grade town centres across the country.

Councillor Bryan Hanson
Leader
Hartlepool Borough Council

Contact: Kate Smith
Landscape & Conservation Manager
Tel. 01429 523413

Rationalise traffic street furniture 11

At Hartlepool civic centre the various categories of street furniture have been reduced to a minimum and painted in a similar colour. This provides a tidy unobtrusive setting for the buildings in the street.

Door

Shop Window Frame

CONTEXT

The terraces of shops along Stanley Road, Bootle were built as three pairs of symmetrically designed blocks facing each other across the road in a very formal layout and design.

The original shopfronts were an integral part of the overall design and conformed to the regular visual rhythm of the terraces.

As the core of the shopping centre moved away, this section of the high street became peripheral and derelict. The street was run down and shopfronts were altered with inappropriate designs and materials. Those shopfronts that had survived were almost obliterated by large out of scale signs. The whole scene gave an impression of decay.

A regeneration programme for the area includes renovating the shopfronts along Stanley Road. Traditional designs and materials have been used to relate visually to the original pattern and character of the complete group of terraces. This is not an attempt to reinstate each of the original designs exactly. Different requirements of traders are met but each shopfront contributes to the new feel of well-being in the street.

At Canterbury a different process is used to achieve a similar effect. The local authority encourages traditional local designs by offering specialist design advice to applicants seeking planning permission. Thus the special character of a particular town centre, which people recognise and admire, is being continued.

Restored shopfronts now complement the design of the group of terraces

Improve shopfronts

12

IMPLEMENTATION AND FUNDING

The work is being carried out as part of the Bootle Maritime City Challenge regeneration programme.

Direct grants of up to 50% were offered to shopkeepers for advice on design and implementation.

Funding was from the City Challenge budget, a central government five year programme. Some businesses have been sufficiently confident to fund their own renovations.

One of our strategic objectives in bidding for City Challenge funding was to help declining local shopping centres.
A measure of success is that businesses with new shopfronts have stayed open.
It has certainly brightened this forgotten part of Bootle and also seems to have reduced street crime.

Councillor Dave Martin
Leader of the Majority Group
Sefton Metropolitan Borough Council

Contact: Steve Power
Economic Programme Manager
Tel. 0151 934 3475

The shopfronts along Stanley Road in a declining area of Bootle are being reinstated in a traditional design which relates visually to the overall character of the terraces. It is part of an overall regeneration scheme.

53

CONTEXT

Shops constantly change hands. Even in prosperous high streets there are usually a few temporarily vacant shops. At the periphery and in less successful centres, empty shops are more common.

In centrally managed shopping centres, vacant shop units are normally boarded or screened with a themed decoration or mural. This prevents them from reducing the attractiveness and viability of the whole centre. Done well, a mural can be a positive asset.

Co-ordination of this kind is more difficult in a high street, because each shop has a different owner or manager. Often when a tenant leaves a shop it is left in an untidy or even derelict state until a new occupier is found.

If a shop is left empty for a long time it can damage the economic viability of the whole street. Flyposters appear, rubbish collects in the shop doorways and the appearance inside the shop windows gradually becomes more unacceptable. Three or four vacant shops could break the essential continuity of a row of shops.

This example shows how the practices of a managed shopping centre can, with some perseverance and ingenuity, be transferred to a high street.

Vacant shopfronts need not spoil a high street. They can be made an asset

IMPLEMENTATION AND FUNDING

The council obtained permission to fix the boards to the vacant shops and they were painted by students of Barnsley College before being put up. The cost was borne by the normal environmental improvement budget.

The illustrations on the boards were influenced by the council's participation in the Britain in Bloom competition.

We were fed up with this derelict old building so we decided to do something. It was certainly an uphill struggle. The previous tenants had left and there was difficulty over the lease which resulted in the whole site deteriorating.
Now, some three years later, it seems likely that the whole building will be refurbished and once more brought back into use.
But during that space of time it was essential that we took the action we did.

Councillor Jeff Ennis
Former Leader of the Council
Barnsley Metropolitan Borough Council

Contact: Archie Sinclair
Principal Planning Officer (Design)
Tel. 01226 772561

Reduce impact of vacant shopfronts 13

Vacant shops opposite the town hall in Church Street, Barnsley have been temporarily faced with bright murals. These show images of Barnsley in Bloom and contribute to the attractiveness of the high street.

CONTEXT

Most high streets have the same national chain stores, all with their own style of shopfront and shopsign. The same collection of standard shopsigns can be seen in any high street throughout the country, so that many high streets have a similar appearance. Extreme examples can completely obliterate the buildings they are attached to. Often any distinguishing characteristic only appears above the level of the shopsigns.

Shopsigns are designed to attract attention. In some places they probably attract too much attention. Making some adjustments to the standard design of corporate signs to suit the individual buildings allows the identity of a street to be more apparent.

The way the lettering and logo are applied and the materials used are most important. A traditional painted sign is often sufficient for the logo to be recognised without dominating the whole building.

As we noted for shopfronts on page 52, if there are styles that are traditional to a particular town centre they should be respected.

Shopsigns including corporate logos can be fitted into the design of the building

IMPLEMENTATION AND FUNDING
The design of shopsigns comes under national planning control.

Standards are more likely to improve if authorities adopt clear policies in their local plans.

We have strict policies about shop signs. The normal logos of many national chain stores are not appropriate when attached as a large sign to an historic building.
We retain original shop signs whenever possible. With new signs, we ensure that corporate logos are appropriate to the design and scale of the whole building.
In my view the policy of relating shop signs to the appearance of the host building should be adopted in all high streets, not just historic centres.

Cllr. Mrs Celia Savage, Chairman
Planning & Development Committee
Waverley Borough Council

Contact: Judith Swift
Central Area Planning Officer
Tel. 01483 869288

Relate shopsigns

Corporate logos can be modified on shopsigns so that the visual quality of the streetscape is not damaged by brash or garish intrusions.

CONTEXT

Building developments often have the potential to raise the quality of urban design in a town centre, for example by sensitively filling a gap in a street frontage.

The first two sketches on the left compare such a development with a typical multi-storey car park. Because of their height and bulk, such car parks are notoriously difficult to fit into a street scene.

At the most mundane level, infill development may be no more than a simple but robust boundary wall at the back of a pavement, hiding an untidy commercial yard.

The lower two sketches demonstrate how simple front garden walls helped prevent a complete street, at the vulnerable edge of a town centre, from becoming run down.

A more elaborate solution, perhaps an infill building which acts as a landmark or a focal point, may be appropriate where a dreary place needs to be brightened up with a powerful, highly visible symbol.

Sensitive infill: whole buildings or simple but robust boundary walls

IMPLEMENTATION AND FUNDING

Action under the housing acts secured the future life of small private houses but also had an economic benefit to the town centre.

Funding was shared between between housing and environmental improvement budgets.

These modest houses back on to a large supermarket car park at the edge of the town centre. Some of the front gardens were a disgrace as the houses were left to decay in the hope of future change of use.
By paying for simple but robust front garden walls and arranging for rear parking spaces, the council made sure that the terrace, which is seen by most visitors to the town centre, was kept tidy. Our action made it clear that the houses were to stay and this encouraged the owners to look after them.

Councillor Frank Cooke
Leader of the Council
London Borough of Bromley

Contact: Robin Cooper
Head of Heritage and Urban Design
Tel. 0181 313 4548

Design infill development   15

New development can knit together gaps in the street scene, mask out of scale structures such as multi-storey car parks or, as these new front garden walls at Bromley show, simply tidy up a vulnerable edge of centre street.

CONTEXT

We are used to seeing boring stretches of pavement along high streets unrelieved by interesting urban spaces.

A new urban space can make a positive contribution to high street character.

This example shows how an inquiring mind and entrepreneurial spirit has converted a shabby recess at the back of the pavement into an asset: a new urban space.

It is the sort of widened pavement which would normally have been overlooked as a potential open space. In many town centres the odd bits of street furniture and equipment would have stayed and the recess would have become a place where more things were dumped: waste recycling bins, control and switch boxes, litter bins, salt bins, odd seats and advertisement drums.

Interesting urban spaces can be created in the most unexpected places

IMPLEMENTATION AND FUNDING
The improvements were the result of
the tenacity of the Notting Hill Gate
Improvements Group. Most of the
costs were borne by each of the agencies
responsible for their own services,
such as pavements, traffic signs and
telephone kiosks.

*We had looked at this widened pavement
for years and then decided to do something about it. Using an idea by a local
architect, Maggie Baynes, we managed
to have the worst traffic signs moved
away completely. Then we relocated the
phone boxes.*
*The Royal Borough of Kensington &
Chelsea certainly played their part.*
*Finally, with the help of Land Securities,
owners of the adjacent office building,
we managed to put up an imposing
wind sculpture by Peter Logan.*
*So we have created a very pleasant
incidental open space from what was
merely an embarrassingly cluttered,
wide pavement.*

John Scott, Co-Founder
Notting Hill Gate Improvements Group

Contact
John Scott   Tel. 0171 221 7722

Create incidental urban space

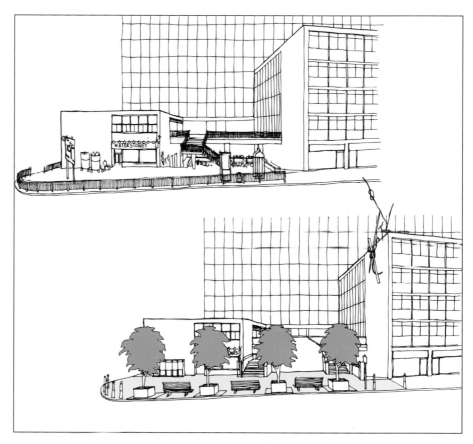

A new and welcome open space has been created at
Notting Hill Gate, London by clearing the clutter from a
widened pavement along a busy high street.

CONTEXT

Trees are an architectural form. Like buildings, they can be positioned to enclose urban space. Unlike buildings, they are living things: they take time to grow so that the effect is seldom immediate.

The presence of trees is usually welcomed. In an urban environment, they can provide movement, colour, contrast and seasonal interest, as well as bringing a distinct quality of light into a street. For planting to be effective in design terms, it must be purposive and take account of the local environment, both built and natural: formal and informal planting of groups and single specimens can be used to add distinctiveness to the high street.

It is also essential that the right tree is planted in the right place. As they mature, some trees can damage property, block out light and obstruct views. With appropriate selection - taking account of potential growth and the characteristics of the tree above and below ground - these problems can be avoided or minimised.

A tree planting and maintenance strategy should follow good arboricultural practice; if pruning, for example, is necessary the basic branch structure should be retained. Trees are appreciated as much in the winter as in the summer, and random lopping can produce a tortured looking appearance in winter.

Street trees: in avenues and groups should be selected to suit their position

IMPLEMENTATION AND FUNDING

The work is carried out as part of the normal maintenance programmes. Pruning is not automatic and only takes place as a result of a specific inspection.

Because they look after so many street trees, the council can afford to retain good arboricultural advice and skills. Funding is from the normal highway maintenance budgets.

We pride ourselves in Cheltenham on the quality of life in our town. Trees contribute to that and we try to keep as many as we can in a shape that people expect to see.
The key to this is in the choice of the right species and the correct position.
Many of our roads are quite wide but when we do plant in narrower streets we use trees with an upright habit and fine foliage, such as birch.

Councillor Mrs Hazel Langford
Chairman of the Trees Sub-committee
Cheltenham Borough Council

Contact: Nick Eden
Trees & Ranger Services Manager
Tel. 01242 250019

Plant street trees

If a tree in Cheltenham needs to be thinned, selected branches are removed from within the canopy in order to retain the tree's overall size, shape and natural appearance.

CONTEXT

Devizes Market Place is an historic urban open space lined with a number of listed buildings. Though at the heart of a country town, the space is essentially urban in character and so permanent, municipal style flower beds would be inappropriate.

Flower baskets provide a splash of colour during the summer. They help mark the seasons. Taking them down in autumn is as important as putting them up in spring. In autumn and winter the Market Place resumes its cool weather character.

The flower baskets are hung from the virtually all the buildings rather than just from lamp posts. Thus they are seen as a mass of colour. This large co-ordinated display of flower baskets is more appropriate in a high street than odd individual baskets and helps to emphasise the completeness of the urban space.

An essential part of the programme is the constant maintenance of the flowers throughout the summer. In some town centres the baskets are put up but not maintained. This can look worse than if there had been no baskets at all.

The Devizes scheme, a contender for the Britain in Bloom award, is successful because it involves most of the traders in the Market Place and has the co-operation of the Chamber of Commerce.

Temporary window boxes and flower baskets bring fresh colour to a high street

IMPLEMENTATION AND FUNDING
Contracts are let each year to provide and water the flowers for hanging baskets and window boxes.

Costs for the baskets, window boxes and administration are shared by the Town Council and the Chamber of Commerce. The nursery contractor then sells his services to individual businesses in the Market Square.

The results are well worth all our effort and expense. The town centre sparkles each summer.
With the local authorities, through the Devizes Partnership, we also make sure that litter is cleared quickly and that buildings are kept in good condition.
People have a choice. We are convinced that they will revisit a town that is attractive and cared for.

Jenny Holt
President, Devizes & District
Chamber of Commerce

Contact: Julian Macdonald
Town Clerk, Devizes Town Council
Tel. 01380 722160

Introduce seasonal colour 18

Flowers create a seasonal splash of colour during the summer. In Devizes, Wiltshire they are placed on almost all the buildings in the Market Place.

CONTEXT

Markets, probably the most basic form of retailing, survive because they offer inexpensive goods. The other attractions are the activity, noise, colour and vitality. They provide a setting for real human interaction, the antidote to supermarket shopping.

Weekly markets bring a sense of occasion to a high street, setting that day apart from the others. Their informality and untidiness are perhaps tolerated because they are temporary. Permanent markets are normally expected to be tidier.

Permanent kiosks are almost self contained shop units and need to be carefully designed, especially if they are free standing and will be seen from all sides, almost as a piece of sculpture. Small individual flower stalls can provide a splash of colour on dreary street corners.

Market stalls: a single barrow, kiosks or regular markets add colour and life

IMPLEMENTATION AND FUNDING
Viable markets are self-financing. Some street market authorities are required to use all the rents for the benefit of the traders and the market.

Major renovation to keep a market healthy may require capital expenditure in addition to normal running costs.

Markets have existed at Wigan since being established under royal charters centuries ago.
They are places where people are not intimidated when they buy such things as a single apple or a small portion.
They are also places which are full of interest, humour and colourful life, not to mention smells and noise.
They are where we expect innovation and perhaps people showing off.
Above all they are places of fun.

Councillor Wilf Brogan
Chairman
Recreation & Amenities Committee
Wigan Metropolitan Borough Council

Contact: Philip Edge
Chief Markets Officer
Tel. 01942 827975

Encourage market stalls and kiosks 19

Markets have been held at Wigan for centuries. Yet they need to be positively managed to prevent decline. Cleanliness and appearance require constant monitoring.

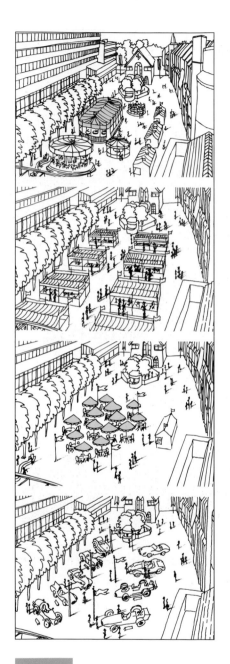

CONTEXT

A town centre is far more than just a shopping centre. It is a place where people gather to meet friends, seek advice, do business, attend concerts, worship, see films, borrow books or just relax.

Urban spaces are places where most of these activities can take place in the open air. As more streets in town centres are made over to pedestrians rather than vehicles, there are more opportunities to treat them as urban spaces and use them for a variety of activities.

The notion that it ought to be possible to relax, sit and talk to your friends or take part in activities without spending money, is attractive.

Although some activities happen spontaneously, an organised programme is needed to ensure continuity, balance, seasonal change and local character.

Town centres usually have urban spaces of different sizes and locations that offer a range of opportunities from local trade promotions, community crafts, society events and productions, through to national special interest festivals and gatherings.

This variety and constant change helps make the town centre complete, interesting and lively as well as commercially attractive and viable.

A high street space used for four different community and commercial activities

Vary activities in urban spaces

20

IMPLEMENTATION AND FUNDING
A City Centre Manager administers a programme of events for the open spaces. He arranges for organisations to hire the pedestrianised areas.

Charges vary according to activity (though the majority are free of charge to encourage community groups). The aim is to provide a variety of attractions while keeping total costs in balance.

People come to Hereford for a day out The town centre is not just a shopping centre, it is a genuine centre for the local community.
At most weekends during the summer we arrange for the pedestrianised High Town to be used for exhibitions, displays and, in this case, a classic car rally.
It gives people a chance to stand around, meet their friends and do more than merely shop.

Councillor John Newman, Chairman Markets, Property & Transport Cttee. Hereford City Council

Contact: Neil Hadley
City Centre Manager
Tel. 01432 364673

The pedestrianised High Town in Hereford has now taken on the character of a town square and is used for a programme of social events such as classic car rallies.

CONTEXT

Town centres are essentially places where people come together. The buildings are a backcloth.

We have discussed urban spaces which can be used for a variety of events. This is a description of an annual event that affects a whole town centre. Surprisingly the English Haydn Festival is held in the small market town of Bridgnorth.

The festival is an important event in the local calendar. For one week each year the series of concerts, recitals, master classes and social events attracts a nationwide audience who would not otherwise visit the town.

The event is seen locally as a positive and regular occasion. It is organised by an independent group and is supported financially by local and national businesses, as well as the three local authorities and national arts foundations.

Hosting a national, if relatively modest and specialist, gathering helps to give the town identity. Most people attending the festival have other interests and apart from patronising local hotels and restaurants, spend time enjoying the town's the other attractions.

Such initiatives rely upon local enthusiasm, although some sort of official recognition and partnership is needed. This may be easier to achieve in a smaller community where there is a network of informal links between different interest groups.

Festivals bring new life and vitality to a town centre

IMPLEMENTATION AND FUNDING
For ten days each June, the Festival Orchestra, Chorus and Ensemble are heard in St. Leonard's Church, the Town Hall and houses in the countryside surrounding the town. The Festival has a growing national and international following.

Organisation is through a voluntary committee, funded by sponsorship from local business, the town, district and county councils, as well as regional and national art foundations.

Bridgnorth Town Council is pleased to support the Festival. It has now expanded from a week to ten days each year and attracts visitors from all over Europe.
It is a tremendous benefit for the town. Hotels and restaurants are fully booked and many people who have been introduced to the town through the Festival come again.

Councillor Judy Lee
The Mayor
Bridgnorth Town Council

Contact: Paddy Harvey
The English Haydn Festival, Bridgnorth
Tel. 01746 766194

Establish special events

The English Haydn Festival at Bridgnorth, Shropshire brings new visitors to the town and contributes to its cultural richness.

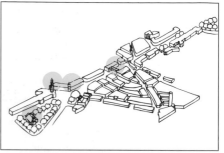

CONTEXT

Most town centres have at least one landmark building or structure which contributes to the character of the place. It need not be historic or even architecturally distinguished; almost anything can be regarded as a landmark if it is sufficiently distinctive or has a significant place in local people's perception of the town centre.

Thus at Brixton, two railway bridges are as much landmarks as the historic church at the end of the high street. The railway bridges are close together but at different levels; they cross the high street almost at its centre and continue as shop arcades or as a high, distinctive viaduct. Rather than being ignored, they are carefully decorated and well maintained as local features.

At a time when there is a tendency towards uniformity and standardisation in traffic signs, street furniture, paving materials, shopfronts and shopsigns, any remaining individuality in a high street should be emphasised. Single landmarks can be accentuated. If there is more than one landmark, the spaces and views between them can be enhanced, so that the group becomes in effect the single landmark for the town centre.

The illustrations on the left show how the tower of the Town Hall at Brixton has been identified as an important landmark. It is being emphasised by the creation of a new incidental urban space in the foreground of the important view from the tube station - in effect one of the entrances to the town centre.

Views of the large street market, also acknowledged as a landmark in the town centre, are seen on page 66.

Landmarks, seen in the distance, are enhanced by improvements to the foreground

72

IMPLEMENTATION AND FUNDING
Buildings identified as contributing to the character of Brixton are eligible for improvement and renovation grants. Most projects have social, environmental and commercial benefits.

Funding is often through the combined resources and financial assistance of the building owner, Lambeth Council, Brixton Challenge Company and English Heritage.

Brixton is a lively place which has a clearly established image.
The co-ordinated programme of regeneration and refurbishment includes improving our landmark buildings and also their settings.
We treat the market as a unique asset. It is the largest Afro-Caribbean market in Europe and as such has a cultural importance which helps to give Brixton an identity of its own.

Councillor Anthony Bays
Mayor
London Borough of Lambeth

Contact: Mel Clinton
Regeneration Officer, Environ. Services
Tel. 0171 926 7171

Accentuate landmarks 22

Landmarks in Brixton and their settings are systematically upgraded. As a group they contribute to the character of the town centre. The street market is so important that it has become a landmark in its own right.

73

CONTEXT

Some places warrant paving of the very best design, materials and workmanship. The Strand in central London is one such. The majority of the buildings are listed or are significant in their own right. The decision was taken to renew the pavements in a style which would be unobtrusive yet contribute to the quality of the street.

Natural York stone and granite were used in their traditional positions as paving, kerbs and crossings for pedestrians. The natural colour of the stone complements the natural stone of the adjacent buildings.

The paving slabs were pre-cut to simple traditional rectangular shapes. Curves at the building line were respected by accurately cut stone. There was no need to add any embellishments or impose a pattern or colour.

In addition many of the pedestrian guard rails were removed. This also eliminated other clutter which tends to be deposited next to guard rails.

Many high streets are laid with small slabs which themselves create an unsatisfactory and cluttered appearance. If the cost of natural stone cannot be justified simple concrete slabs, well laid to a considered design, are usually acceptable (see page 46).

The granite setts shown on the left are particularly effective because the yellow lines have been removed and replaced by unobtrusive signs (see page 47).

Attempts to introduce brightness by patterned or artificially coloured paving materials are seldom satisfactory. Apart from the problems of maintenance and construction, the valuable function of a pavement as a unifying element in a high street is lost.

Quality paving often succeeds if it is unobtrusive with no added embellishment

IMPLEMENTATION AND FUNDING
The new paving is part of a scheme to rationalise local traffic patterns and give greater priority to public transport. It was paid for by Westminster City Council with contributions from local businesses.

Once described by Disraeli as 'perhaps the finest street in Europe', over recent years the appearance of the Strand has deteriorated. In order to restore some of its grandeur we are introducing the highest quality improvements including widening and repaving pavements, closing some side roads and improving street furniture and lighting. Improvements to the appearance of buildings are also being promoted with the Civic Trust in association with the frontagers of the Strand.
The scheme is producing a much more attractive townscape and is giving the area a greater air of confidence and encouraging investment in the street.

Councillor Alan Bradley, Chairman
Planning and Environment Committee
City of Westminster

Contact: Malcolm Haxby
Assistant Corporate Director (Policy)
Tel. 0171 798 2923

The pavements of the Strand, London are being refurbished to the highest standards. A simple design of natural stone is being used.

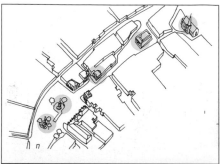

CONTEXT

Town centres have many attractions at night. They take on different characteristics and may be used by different people. Unlike shopping centres, their activities extend into the hours of darkness all year and in some places all through the night.

Whereas street lighting is intended for safety and convenience, public lighting gives the opportunity to accentuate important buildings, spaces and activities. Distant views or monuments can be given greater emphasis. Contrasting shadows and unlit areas can create an almost magical effect.

A public lighting strategy can be undertaken as part of a town centre analysis. Important buildings, landmarks, vistas and enclosed spaces, a distant church spire, formal set piece architectural statements such as a group of civic buildings or incidental open spaces leading off a high street can all be lit as part of an overall strategy.

Although floodlit buildings are quite common, a public lighting strategy for an entire town centre is more unusual and requires considerable effort. Normally buildings are lit according to the inclination of the individual owner. Whereas a single building may look attractive the total scene may not necessarily attain its full potential. Architecturally or socially important buildings may not necessarily have owners either willing or able to undertake a lighting scheme. Some buildings may need to be visually subdued in order to achieve an overall effect.

The Leeds Lighting Initiative, launched in 1993, has largely resolved these practical difficulties. Its objects are to improve the quality and visual appeal of the city. A lighting strategy for the city centre was produced by lighting consultants and is used to promote co-ordinated schemes through grants and encourage good practice through awards.

A lighting strategy, based on a town centre analysis, can have a magical effect

IMPLEMENTATION AND FUNDING

Schemes selected within the Lighting Initiative are offered up to 50% grants for the design and implementation of lighting. Running costs are borne by the building owner. An award is also given for good lighting schemes throughout Leeds.

In 1996, £250,000 was spent in the City centre on environmental improvements; of this, approximately half was for lighting grants.

The Leeds Lighting Initiative is part of a public and private sector partnership to develop Leeds as a major European centre ready to meet the challenges of the next century.

Our Lighting Code of Practice seeks to ensure that all lighting schemes are aesthetically pleasing and energy efficient and also result in minimum pollution of the night sky.

Councillor Brian Walker
Leader
Leeds City Council

Contact: Peter Vaughan
Environmental Design Officer
Tel. 0113 247 8140

Install public lighting

24

A public lighting initiative at Leeds uses grants and awards to encourage owners of buildings to light their buildings effectively. The Town Hall sets an example.

CONTEXT

The term art in public places usually brings to mind sculptures or murals rather than the decoration which is present in various forms in every high street. Sculpture tends to draw attention to itself and is therefore often positioned where it can act as a focal point. Murals are frequently seen on blank walls, perhaps at the end of a terrace.

Decoration is present in the architectural detail of landmark buildings, churches, town halls, public houses and in changing shop window displays.

To be successful, new art in the high street should relate to what is already there. It should contribute to existing visual themes and character and not be added for the sake of it, without adequate reference to its context.

As communities become more familiar with applied art, they may accept more adventurous examples. The following list gives an idea of the breadth of alternatives.

Art can:
  be humorous
  be figurative
  be available to a wide audience
  be walked through as well as round
  be temporary as well as permanent
  be tactile and robust
  be audible
  be commemorative
  have local associations
  project civic pride and
  lift the spirits.

Art and decoration are present in various forms in every high street

25

IMPLEMENTATION AND FUNDING

The sculptures in Blandford Street, commissioned in 1991 from the artist Matthew Jarett, were put up by the City Council in partnership with a local organisation, Art Resource. They are fixed to a row of double lamp columns in the centre of the pedestrianised street.

Funding was through the a combination of Urban Programme and EU funds.

We were keen to have a reminder of the City's fishing and shipping industries in the town centre. These sculptures have been well received by the people of Sunderland as many local families were employed in activities connected with the sea.
Because of their robust construction the images seem as fresh now as when they were first put up.

Councillor Malcolm Qualie
Chair of the Environment Committee
City of Sunderland

Contact: Keith Hamilton
Design and Conservation Manager
Tel. 0191 553 1514

Silhouette sculptures are placed at well above head height and at regular intervals along Blandford Street, Sunderland. They depict the former seafaring trades and industries of the city.

The Royal Fine Art Commission

Chairman
The Right Honourable the Lord St John
of Fawsley PC FRSL Hon FRIBA

Members
Miss Sophie Andreae MA
Professor R David Carter CBE RDI
Edward Cullinan Esq CBE RA BA AADip
    RIBA Hon FRIAS
Sir Philip Dowson CBE MA PRA AADip RIBA
Donald Hamilton Fraser Esq RA
Edmund Hollinghurst Esq MA CEng FICE
    FIStructE FIHT
Sir Michael Hopkins CBE RA AADip RIBA
Stuart Lipton Esq Hon RIBA
Professor Margaret MacKeith MA PhD FRTPI
Hal Moggridge Esq OBE PPLI RIBA AADip
Mrs John Nutting JP
Trevor Osborne Esq FRICS
Ian Ritchie Esq Dip Arch PCL RIBA FRSA
Professor John Steer MA D Litt FSA
Miss Wendy Taylor CBE LDAD FZS FQMW
Quinlan Terry Esq FRIBA
Dr Giles Worsley MA PhD

7 St. James's Square
London SW1Y 4JU
Tel. 0171 839 6537

Colin J Davis & Associates
23 Southwood Gardens
Esher KT10 ODF
Tel. 0181 398 7837

Acknowledgements

Members of the
Improving Design in the High Street Steering Group

Francis Golding, Chairman	Royal Fine Art Commission
Michael Bach	Department of the Environment
Robert Bargery	Royal Fine Art Commission
Richard Coleman	Royal Fine Art Commission
Colin Davis	Colin J Davis & Associates
Professor Margaret MacKeith	Royal Fine Art Commission
Robert Pearce	Marks & Spencer
Richard Pullen	Department of the Environment
Keith Redshaw	Land Securities

The group wishes thank all those people mentioned in Part III who agreed to send a personal message from their authorities or organisations. Thank you also to those who agreed to act as contacts, for your time in helping to produce this book

The Royal Fine Art Commission is grateful to
Department of the Environment
Land Securities
Marks & Spencer

Designed and illustrated by
Colin Davis, William Spencer and Michael Robinson

Photographs on the following pages were kindly lent by the respective authorities: pages 43, 45, 47, 58, 63, 66 and 77. The photographs on page 33 were lent by Simons Design, Lincoln, on pages 35, 64 and 65 by Norman Ellis ARPS, on page 71 by the English Haydn Festival and on page 74 by W S Atkins Planning Consultants